Uplifting the Soul Through Poetry

by Shirley Adley

Forward

In I Peter 4:10-11 the scriptures tell us that God has granted each of us a special gift. How we use this gift is our choice. We must use it wisely, serving others, and thus glorifying God. I thank God for the gift to put my thoughts into poetry. My prayer is that this book of poems will touch you're heart, change you're life, and bring you closer to God.

Acknowledgements

I give thanks to God for the gift he gave me to express my thoughts into poems. I wish to thank my whole family for all the encouraging words they expressed everytime I would read them one of my poems.
I especially wish to thank my daughter-in-law Becky Conners for the endless hours she put in on the computer, helping me edit this book, and getting it formatted for publishing. Without her help I could not have accomplished this task.

Ecstasy

I wrote this poem in January 1964 in the backseat of my family's car. We were moving from Ft.Worth Texas to Tillamook Oregon. My Dad had taken a job as a minister for the Church of Christ in Tillamook. I was excited about moving to another state and helping the church grow in Tillamook. But I was also sad because I was leaving my fiancée behind, even though he would be joining us in a few months. It was these mixed emotions that helped me create this thought provoking poem.

*"Love suffers long and is kind; love does not envy;
love does not parade itself; is not puffed up;
does not behave rudely, does not seek its own,
Is not provoked, thinks no evil; does not rejoice in iniquity,
but rejoices in the truth; bears all things, believes all things,
hopes all things, endures all things.
Love never fails."*

I CORINTHIANS 13: 4-8

Ecstasy

How many petals of roses should fall,
to open the door of life to us all?
The golden leaves of autumn that fall to the ground
tells us life's passing, quick, look around.
But spring will come and with it hope to help us in our strife,
then and only then we'll know that this is truly life.

Take my hand and lead me down that narrow path you trod.
Let's build a life together around the love of God.
Where you go I'll follow till death makes us part,
but even then you can be sure I'll hug you in my heart.
For now let's walk together, talk together, lift our eyes above,
then and only then we'll know that this is truly love.

Show me all the loveliness of life there is to see.
The summer breeze will tease our hair and say, "Come play with me."
Count the many colors in the rainbow one by one.
Hold me close at evening as we watch the setting sun.
Imagine all the beauty that lies beyond the sea,
for this is life and this is love and both are ecstasy.

Whispers

This poem is about a 96 year old woman who has outlived all her husbands and children, and this is her last plea to God.

*"Is anyone among you suffering?
Let him pray."*
*"The effective fervent prayer
of a righteous
man avails much."*

JAMES 5:13,16

"We finish our years like a sigh."

PSALM 90:9

Whispers

Her arthritic body settles in the rocking chair
as her mind drifts back to times when her family was all there.
She asks herself this question, "Did I do my very best
in raising up my children...did I pass the test?"
And he whispers, " Yes...you did."

She lays a hand upon her brow
and says a silent prayer,
"Lord, my bones are tired and now I'm old
does anybody care?"
And he whispers, " Yes...I care."

She sips her tea beside the fire
and watches the embers glow.
"How long ,Oh Lord , must I remain
down here on this earth below?"
My eyes are weak, my hearings gone
and the hands are so unsteady.
She bows her head, her eyes are closed
and she sighs... am I ready?
And he whispers, "Yes...Come home."

This Moment In Time

Living in Colorado has given me such an appreciation for the beauty God has showered upon this state. This poem was inspired by an actual event.

"He has made everything beautiful in it's time."

ECCLESIASTES 3:11

This Moment In Time

Gently, I walked through a meadow this morning
just as the sun was beginning to rise.
I was humming a hymn I learned in my childhood
when an array of beauty fell before my eyes.

I sat on a rock up under the pine trees
and breathed in the air so sublime.
"Thank you Lord," I whispered, "for this beautiful day
but especially this moment in time."

The various hues that laid out before me
just took my breath away.
They call it the bear grass, but it's really a lily,
the palest of yellows I'd say.

The red Indian paintbrushes and lavender asters
brought the scent of rosemary and thyme.
Lord thank you for leading me here this morning
to experience this moment in time.

I Stand In Awe

The first time I saw the clouds kiss the mountains, I was speechless. After that, I was eager to witness this remarkable beauty over and over again. One morning, as I was driving home from work, I saw it again. As tears filled my eyes I began to pray. This was my prayer.

*"Let all the earth fear the Lord;
let all the inhabitants of the world
stand in Awe of him."*

PSALM 33:8

I Stand In Awe

Father, when I see
the clouds kiss the mountains,
I stand in awe of the
beauty you have bestowed
upon this earth.
I feel so small in this vast
universe you have created.
But I know I must be important to you,
since you created mankind in you're image.
I love you Lord with every
fiber of my being.
Thank you for loving me and
sending your son to die for my sins
so that we may all live together
someday in heaven.

The Choice

I wrote this poem in memory of my nephew Brad Bruce. He was taken from this life on November 18, 2004. He was only 18 years old.

*"Whereas you do not know what will happen tomorrow.
For what is your life?
It is even a vapor that appears for a little time
and then vanishes away."*

JAMES 4:14

The Choice

The teacher asked the students
if you had the choice to make,
to take one soul to heaven
just who would you choose to take?

My nephew's turn came to answer,
he spoke up with a calming voice,
"I couldn't choose just one you see,
I'd have to take you all with me.
Yes, that would be my choice."

A few weeks later his soul went to God.
His body is buried beneath the sod.
His life was but a vapor that vanished away.
We need to ask ourselves, "are we ready to die today?"

God knew he lived to serve others,
the day he took him home.
There on his marker is revealed
the plan of salvation…chiseled in stone.

When God Calls You Home

Questions to ponder…questions to answer.

" ...for I was hungry and you gave Me food;
I was thirsty and you gave Me drink;
I was a stranger and you took me in;
I was naked and you clothed Me;
I was sick and you visited Me;
I was in prison and you came to Me."
"...assuredly, I say to you,
in as much as you did it to one of the least of these
My brethren, you did it to Me."

MATTHEW 25: 35-36 & 40

" As I live, says the Lord, every knee shall bow to Me,
and every tongue shall confess to God."

ROMANS 14:11

When God Calls You Home

When God calls you home are you ready?
Has you're life been worthy and good?
Have you tended the sick, given alms to the poor,
provided comfort the way that you should?

Will God find you unworthy but wanting
to enter the promise land?
Have you said no to a friend who was in need,
or did you lend a helping hand?

When God calls you home are you ready?
Is you're life fulfilled and complete?
Take heed my friend, the time is near
we will all have to answer at the judgment seat.

A Home Without God

With all the abuse in the world today, I felt compelled to write a poem encouraging parents to cherish the greatest gift God will ever give them..... their children.

*" Train up a child in the way he should go,
and when he is old he will not
depart from it."*

PROVERBS 22:6

A Home Without God

*Imagine if you will a home without God,
no laughter or singing is heard.
A little child cries alone in his room,
his daddy walked out without a word.*

*His mother is passed out there on her bed
from all the boozing and drugs.
A little child cries alone in his room
longing for kisses and hugs.*

*No one can hear him, nobody cares,
hours and days passes by.
Now there's a child alone in his room
too weak to even cry.*

*Parents please cherish
this gift from above,
and raise you're sweet children
in a house full of love.*

*Never neglect them, never forget them,
show them you love them each day.
Tell them about Jesus and God's sweet love
and teach them how to pray.*

Beacon Of Light

In the midst of apprehension, one finds peace.

*"The eyes of the Lord are on the righteous,
and his ears are open to their cry."*

PSALM 34:15

Beacon Of Light

The sun hangs low on the horizon,
as the ocean waves crest higher.
She sits on the edge of the cliff
warming herself by the fire.

He left out early this morning
in a boat they had owned for two years.
He should have been back hours ago,
she asks God to allay her fears.

She cries out, "Oh Father please protect him,
bring him home safely to me."
As the last light of day fades to darkness,
her eyes searches the waves of the sea.

She keeps adding more wood to the fire,
like a beacon in the night.
Then she hears a faint voice calling,
"I can see the light."

She falls on her knees and gives thanks,
to the good Lord up above,
for allowing this beacon of light
to guide home her one true love.

My Angel

This was a true experience that I shall never forget

*"The angel of the Lord encamps
all around those who fear him and delivers them."*

PSALM 34:7

My Angel

I believe we have an angel
watching over us each day.
From the time we're little babies
until the hour we pass away.

You see, one day I saw my angel
and it took me by surprise.
But a calming peace filled my soul
as I gazed into his eyes.

His face was extraordinarily beautiful,
I recall that thought in my mind.
No words were exchanged or movements made
but his smile was so warm and kind.

Yes, I believe in angels
and since that day I'm not the same.
Time stood still for a moment
and I never knew his name.

Remember

Lest you forget…

"Father, if it is Your will, take this cup from Me; nevertheless not My will, but Yours be done."
"Then an angel appeared to Him from heaven, strengthening Him. And being in agony, He prayed more earnestly. Then His sweat became like great drops of blood falling to the ground."

LUKE 22:42-44

Remember

Take the time to clear you're mind
from all this worldly strife,
When you partake of communion on Sundays
remember our Saviors life.

Take thought to his kneeling in the garden,
with great drops of sweat falling from his face.
When you partake of communion on Sundays
remember his saving grace.

"Father please forgive them,"
he said with his dying breath.
When you partake of communion on Sundays
remember our Saviors death.

Take It To The Lord In Prayer

In the midst of confusion, one finds clarity

"Be anxious for nothing, but in everything, by prayer and supplication, with thanksgiving, let your request be made known to God."

PHILIPPIANS 4:6

Take It To The Lord In Prayer

Sometimes the struggles in our life
seems impossible to bear.
We obey the commandments and the laws of the land,
but our problems are always there.

When that mountain gets higher than you can climb,
and no one around seems to care.
To allay all you're worries and bring peace to your soul,
take it to the Lord in prayer.

The scriptures say ask and you shall receive
to seek and you shall find.
Let go of you're worries and put them in His pocket,
then leave them all behind.

Be assured that you have
a friend who will care,
by taking you're concerns
to the Lord in prayer.

Katie

This poem is dedicated to my late husband Lee. He and Katie were inseparable

"I thank God upon every remembrance of you."

PHILIPPIANS 1:3

Katie

I never wanted much in life;
a home, some kids, a loving wife.
It didn't happen overnight,
it took some years to get it right.
...and then we got a dog.

We adopted her from the animal shelter,
we named her Katie which seemed to fit her.
She had endless energy day and night
with a huge voracious appetite.

When football games come on t.v.
she grabs her ball and brings it to me.
For the next three hours it's two-three hut,
she's such a silly little mutt.

She's eleven now and has my heart.
I know someday we'll have to part.
She's my shadow and a true companion to me,
thank you Lord, for my friend Katie.

Things My Children Love

Moments to cherish

"Behold, children are a heritage from the Lord."

PSALM 127:3

Things My Children Love

Skipping rocks across the lake
Chasing fireflies in the night
Playing tag and jumping rope
The smell of bacon at first light.

Taking bubble baths each night
Having good old pillow fights
On their knees praying to God above
These are the things my children love.

The Walk

Walking with God is good for the heart...

"And the peace of God, which surpasses all understanding, will guard your hearts and minds through Christ Jesus."

Philippians 4:7

The Walk

Take a walk with me today
on a path I've chosen.
Down the lane and through the woods
to a stream that's frozen.

Do you see beneath the ice
the undercurrent flowing?
And over there behind that rock
the rainbow trout are glowing.

Sitting here upon this rock
with you by my side,
I feel content, an inner peace,
and a love I cannot hide.

Thank you for this walk today
it meant alot to me,
To have you Lord there by my side
to share the things I see.

The Hills Of Virginia

Contentment brings happiness to the soul.

*" Not that I speak in regard to need,
for I have learned in whatever state I am,
to be content."*

PHILIPPIANS 4:11

The Hills Of Virginia

*Her cabin is small but efficient,
she keeps it as neat as a pin.
She hums to herself in the kitchen,
while she bastes the Cornish hen.*

*The woods that surround her home place
are mysteriously quiet at times.
But she was raised in these hills of Virginia,
when her Papa worked down in the mines.*

*She's chosen to live out her life here,
free from life's struggles and strife.
Yes, here in the hills of Virginia
lives a woman content with her life.*

Impact

You will always remember the kindness of others.

*" And be kind to one another,
tenderhearted,
forgiving one another,
even as God in Christ forgave you."*

EPHESIANS 4:32

Impact

We never know what impact
we may have on someone's life.
A smile, a touch, or just a kind word
can take away their strife.

It doesn't take much effort
and it won't cost you a dime.
Try it today on a stranger
it may change their life in time.

Bridging The Gap Between Time

Sometimes an old song can spark a precious memory.

" I thank God upon every remembrance of you."

PHILIPPIANS 1:3

Bridging The Gap Between Time

*Isn't it funny when a golden oldie
starts playing on the radio,
it instantly conjures up a memory
of long, long ago.
Like a grandfather clock ready to chime
bridging the gap between time.*

*All at once you're transformed to a place
so precious only two hearts could understand.
Watching the moon shimmer across the water,
walking down the beach hand in hand.*

*So many years since that special moment,
and it's never been far from my mind.
But that song on the radio brings a smile to my face,
bridging the gap between time.*

Because He Loved Us So

Jesus paid the ultimate price for you and me…and he did it with love.

*" This is My commandment,
that you love one another as I have loved you."
" Greater love has no one than this,
than to lay down one's life for his friends."*

JOHN 15:12-13

Because He Loved Us So

He left the security of Heaven
to enter this world of sin.
He wanted to reveal the truth
and change the lives of men.

The words in the Bible, that are printed in red,
are so important for us to know.
Yes, he came and gave us his promise,
because he loved us so.

They beat his body and scorned him,
and placed thorns upon his head.
Not for a crime he had committed,
but for the life he had led.

So there he was crucified up on that cross
over two thousand years ago,
but he was willing to die for all of our sins,
because he loved us so.

God Chose You

Death is but a resting stop between Earth and Heaven.

" *Let not your heart be troubled;
you believe in God,
believe also in Me.
In My Father's house are many mansions;
if it were not so, I would have told you.
I go to prepare a place for you…
that where I am you may be also.*"

JOHN 14:1-3

God Chose You

God chose you to go before me,
leaving me to walk alone.
In a world that's ever changing
for my sins to atone.

Saying good-bye to you dear one
was the hardest thing I've done.
I'm now alone to walk this earth
but my journey's just begun.

God chose you to go before me
for a reason all his own.
But we'll be together someday
in our heavenly Father's home.

Night Sounds

This poem was inspired by a memory of one summer night, long ago.

*" Day unto day utters speech,
and night unto night reveals knowledge."*

PSALM 19:2

Night Sounds

The night is warm and the window's open,
I close my eyes and listen.
The sounds of the night that fills my soul
makes my Spirit glisten.

I hear the call of the Whippoorwill
in the woods down by the lake.
He sounds so sad, I know not why,
he's calling for his mate.

As crickets chirp and frogs keep croaking,
I smile as I hear one more.
The most precious sound I hear at night
is my daddy's undeniable snore.

Walking With God

With God as you're co-pilot, you're never alone.

"And my God shall supply all your needs according to his riches in glory by Christ Jesus."

Philippians 4:19

Walking With God

I'm walking down this road with God,
not knowing where we'll go.
My trust in him is so complete
no fear will I show.

He opens doors throughout my life,
blindly I enter in.
Because he knows what's best for me,
I question not why or when.

He carries me when my bones are tired,
and lights my path when my eyes are dim.
I'm walking down this road with God,
he's taking me home with him.

Heaven Only Knows

God will sustain you, in you're time of grief.

"The Lord is near to those who have a broken heart."

PSALM 34:18

Heaven Only Knows

Heaven only knows
the sadness in my heart.
The loneliness I feel
since we've been apart.

My prayers go up as incense
to the mighty Lord above.
I ask that he take care of you
and wrap you in his love.

Heaven only knows
how hard it is to stay
behind and live my life
away from you each day.

Someday we'll be together,
when at last my eyelids close.
Not knowing when that hour may be,
cause heaven only knows.

Moments Shared

Hold close to your heart the memories of you're children.

" And he lifted his eyes and saw the women and children, and said," who are these with you?"
So he said, "The children whom God has graciously given your servant."

GENESIS 33:5

Moments Shared

I peaked out my window overlooking the lake
and saw a most precious sight.
Paper and sticks and strings in their hands,
the boys were building a kite.

The oldest one took control right away
saying, "This is the way we can do it."
He fumbles and struggles to stretch out the paper
to make the framework fit.

I noticed my younger son there on his knees,
watching his brother intensely.
He spoke not a word soaking everything in,
he admired his brother immensely.

At last it was finished and a site to behold,
the moment of truth was suspenseful.
A tear filled my eye when I saw the kite fly
and I realized I just shared something wonderful.

Laundry Day

Letting go is never easy

*" And now abide faith, hope, and love,
these three; but the greatest of these is love."*

I CORINTHIANS 13:13

Laundry Day

As I sort through the laundry
separating the socks from the jeans,
I ask myself this question,
"Are my children really teens?"

Where have all the years gone...
they were babies yesterday.
It won't be long
they'll test their wings,
and someday fly away.

Roads

Life is but a journey down many roads.

*"The highway of the upright is to depart from evil;
He who keeps his way preserves his soul."*

PROVERBS 16:17

Roads

We wonder through life down many roads,
not knowing which way to turn.
The decision's we make with every turn we take
are lessons we have to learn.

The road to the left may be bumpy and hard,
we struggle our whole life through.
The road to the right may be easy and soft
where all of our dreams come true.

But, not choosing a road leaves us lost and alone,
so choose wisely my friend and tread on.
It matters not what we take to the end of the road,
but what we leave behind when we're gone.

The Fishing Trip

This poem was inspired after one of my sons fishing trips.

" Ask and it will be given to you."

LUKE 11:9

The Fishing Trip

He carefully loaded up the boat
with his tackle box and bait.
He took an extra jacket along
in case he stayed out late.

He heard the walleye were biting,
his anticipation rising high.
He trolled the lake from one end to the other
as the sun set low in the sky.

All of a sudden he saw his pole bend.
He grabbed up the rod to reel the line in.
And as he was struggling he said a prayer to God,
"Lord don't let this one be another log."
Finally he pulled it up into the boat,
exhausted and tired but elated.
A sixteen pound walleye laying there at his feet
was more than he ever anticipated.

Take Me With Her

Imagine all the possibilities in the power of prayer.

" *For If we live , we live to the Lord;*
and if we die, we die to the Lord.
So, whether we live or die, we belong to the Lord."

ROMANS 14:8

Take Me With Her

He patted her hand as he held it,
not wanting to ever let go.
His heart was slowly breaking,
because he loved her so.

He prayed long and hard and earnestly,
trying to keep his repose.
He cried out, "Oh Father, please Father,
take me with her when she goes."

"We've been together every day
for sixty-two sweet years.
She's been my strength throughout my life,"
he said, wiping away the tears.

He was still by her side the next morning,
hand in hand with a smile on his face.
Yes, his prayers were heard and answered
through our heavenly Father's grace.

To Order Copies of

Uplifting the Soul Through Poetry

by **Shirley Adley**

I.S.B.N. 1-59879-155-9

Order Online at:
www.authorstobelievein.com

By Phone Toll Free at:
1-877-843-1007